# SHARDS
# OF LIGHT

Emyr Humphreys

UNIVERSITY OF WALES PRESS

2018

*www.uwp.co.uk*

*Shards of Light*
by Emyr Humphreys
poems collected and edited by Dewi Humphreys
cover image by Guto Humphreys

*British Library CIP Data*
A catalogue record for this book is available from the British Library.

ISBN        978-1-78683-351-8
eISBN       978-1-78683-352-5

The right of Emyr Humphreys to be identified as author of this work has been asserted in accordance with sections 77 and 79 of the Copyright, Designs and Patents Act 1988.

The publisher acknowledges the financial support of the Welsh Books Council.

Typeset by Marie Doherty
Printed by CPI Antony Rowe, Melksham, Wiltshire

# CONTENTS

# INTRODUCTION

It is twenty years since I assisted Emyr Humphreys in preparing his *Collected Poems*. He had already reached his eightieth birthday, and little did I then think that over the following two decades he would somehow succeed in producing another set of powerful poems that would merit publication to celebrate his hundredth birthday.

*Emyr Humphreys: novelist*. Obviously. Over a writing career spanning some sixty years he has published more than two dozen novels, several of them award-winning and including both the greatest English-language novel yet written about Wales (*Outside the House of Baal*, 1965) and a remarkable definitive sequence of seven novels encompassing the 'Welsh experience' throughout much of the twentieth century (*The Land of the Living*, 1971–91). There are, therefore, few who would be inclined to dispute that he is modern Wales's most distinguished writer of fiction.

But *Emyr Humphreys: poet*? Such a description is very likely to raise eyebrows, and yet it was the aspiration to be a poet that first prompted him to become a writer, way back at the end of the 1930s. Indeed, his best-known novel (*A Toy Epic*, which won him the prestigious Hawthornden Prize in 1958) had actually started life two decades earlier as the beginnings of a long autobiographical poem. Moreover, when his striking poetic sequence entitled *Ancestor Worship* appeared in 1970, it was immediately evident that in Humphreys post-war Wales had a poet of truly original, indeed singular, talent. His was a kind of poetry totally unlike that of any of his contemporaries. And the poems in the present volume continue to arrest, and indeed to startle, precisely because they are so unusual.

In some cases, their unorthodox character could clearly be said to owe much to Humphreys's gifts as a novelist. In shrewd social portraits, such as that of an old Italian peasant woman's bewildered dislike of her aggressive daughter-in-law, can be discerned the same qualities that make his novels so distinctive. They are unsparing in their dispassionate dissection of character and situation. He has always been mindful of the observation of his early mentor, Graham Greene, that a novelist should retain a chip of ice in the brain.

Humphreys's poems are characterised by their cool, measured calibrations of experience. His is a poetry characterised by an absence of ego-concern and a willingness to recognise that one's own face is simply one in an infinite ocean of faces. Just as anyone's merely human being is an insignificant existence amidst the irreduceable 'otherness' of an unimagineably vast, mysterious universe, although it is none the less remarkable and precious for being so:

> Ultimate discoveries
> Are made in winter
> Snow on the piste
> And galaxies piercing the sky
> Pin pricks in the velvet
> Choreograph small lives

It is under such conditions that one perceives

> a spider's thread
> Of existence suspended
> Like a piece of debris in outer space
> That intermittently catches the sun
> And threatens the sky with
> The glitter of inexplicable messages.

From time to time there shyly surfaces an awed acknowledgement of a dimension of reality forever beyond human comprehension, one that is sometimes to be intuited haunting the limits of language and fleetingly manifest in the non-human world. 'Grass in all its forms,' he writes, 'Insists on singing just as / Nettles sting,' and, for Humphreys, palpably evident in creation is the 'votive urge towards eternity.' In the face of that which will never yield to the importuning of language, Humphreys has always recognised himself in Wittgenstein's strictures on the need to keep silent. And his repeated vulnerability to wonder, even in extreme old age, is constantly moving. 'Blood,' he writes, 'Provides me with / An indefinable rejoicing / But no words yet / To encompass the explosion.'

Like his great long-standing friend R. S. Thomas, Humphreys is convinced that poetry can take us closest to whatever ultimately *is*, and in one of several poems addressing the unique modus operandi of poetry, he has noted how

> Between words as between lovers
> There are hesitations that
> Mean as much if not more
> Than the coloured links
> In the chain

He is accordingly spare in his deployment of language, and many of the poems are so cerebral and condensed, and so lapidary, that they seem to aspire to the condition of epigram. The writing undoubtedly owes something to that of such admired Italian models as Montale, and above all to the lucid complexities of the sublime Dante of whom Humphreys is a devoted reader. But it is also reminiscent of the great pithy poetry of the Welsh strict-metre tradition, which, like that of Humphreys, can sometimes be suggestively riddling.

Although his visits to the past are remarkably restrained, for one of such advanced years ('All that afternoon I lived / in the nineteen thirties . . .'), episodes from his large storehouse of experiences are occasionally clearly recycled in a compendious poetry that is thus able to apprehend refugee experience, the malign power and appeal of dictators, the fragile egos of the acting profession, the scholarly devotees of Etruscan remains, the contemporaneity of legends from the Mabinogion. On some subjects, such as the obsession with wealth and power, Humphreys is coolly tart. But wry and scathingly sardonic though he can be — a reminder that in his fiction he is a first-class satirist — he is never merely cynical or sour. And only very rarely, in his darkest hour, does he confess to knowing the temptation to despair.

Most affecting, however, is his short, heart-breakingly equable meditation on the loss of his wife and beloved soul-mate, Elinor, at the end of sixty years of married life:

And in this only lies our hope
My dear our so called undying affection
Is the mote in the beam
Of this love that controls the planet
And holds the sun in its place.

Our love was comforting
So why should you go before me?
Even a withered leaf has form
Beautiful when held up to the sun.

# SHARDS
# OF LIGHT

# WE ARE OLD AGE

We are old age, look
At us closely and study
Your reflection precise
As bank statements your years'
Accounts are registered in our
Wrinkles – fruit in store
Shrinks unless eaten
The past is to be consumed the
Future has vague promise but
Less nourishment.

Death is like the stars
It lives in darkness hovers
Above our heads with patient
Benevolence like a farmer
Who feeds his animals
With a fatherly affection
And sighs when the time comes
To carry them to the slaughterhouse.

# SCRATCHES ON STONE

Poetry begins and ends in a cellar
Nothing I have written was worth writing
Say the scratches on the stone
The battle raged the guerrillas won
And in a matter of weeks turned their guns
Against each other who could the poet
Sing to? Only the blank walls of his cell
Only the vibrating membrane between his
Brain as it bled and his mind as it
Continued to reverberate
After the explosion devour itself.

# BLUEBELLS

Mankind with all the world's alarms
Does not suffer in silence. Unlike bluebells
When trodden talks not when taped.
They respond with anything from music to
Unheard screams. A man who does not suffer
Has lived in boots that never touched
The ground he has no right to speak.
Unlike lilies of the field or rubble
Respond in sighs and screams.

With all the world's alarms
And miseries alive in two dimensions
Pressing in, how do you account
Compute find the clue the cloak in the mist
Your survival. Feet like imperial boots
Have never touched the ground and from the royal box
Suck hemlock in the golden bowl.

How to put flesh

Back on the bone

No problem

The expert was deft as a joke

I can make lips

That never whistle

The only ones

You can say with safety

Resurrect without

Burning fingers

Must be

Safely dead.

Sunlight must mean more

Than something seen

For the second time

Below the neck

From frozen shoulder

To feet of clay

Nothing moves.

Inside the skull

Is darker than

A dead planet

Until you touch

Celestial fire

And the whole earth sings

As it burns.

So we keep trying
Something will give
In the sense that grace is given
In order that septic fingers
Turn clay into flesh

And a pretty girl
Emerges beyond dancing
A desperate witch
Tied to a burning wheel.

# CHILDHOOD

Enchanting is the word they use to describe such children

*Hudolus* – and it is correct

They come from a fifth dimension

Inhabited by animals and fairies

Unprotected by social hours

Or flights of adult fancy

When seconds are extended

To enclose not mere universal smiles

But contentments of containment

Nuts like nuggets of untampered time

Functions of living endowed with

Ceremonies from the stars

And ancient certainties as new as buds

Or rings on little fingers.

# LAMENT FOR A GAME OF COWBOYS AND INDIANS

Small as a top in the square back garden
I fished for Time with a broken stick
As if the breeze that stroked my cheek would harden
Or upstairs, after dark, the flame solidify upon its wick.

White-kneed, cap crooked, one arm encircling
The warm neck of a terrier named 'No more'
I want back the swarm of afternoons that swallowed our adventure
Wrapped in the old roller-towel behind the kitchen door.

Eddie Paleface drop that hat and mister
Pick up your tomahawk and raid the hill
Where the palaeolithic cavern drips with treasure
No thief can empty and no clock can fill.

Here is the hill but you and I have gone.
Our trikes have vanished, our chiefs passed on.

The backward glance – the ruined mill
The watercress that clogs the stream
The leaves of urgent spring and those
Footsteps in the green mud – the worthless
Urge to hold the moment, as elusive
As sunlight in the lane.

Between mice and men
There needs to be an understanding
A writ of habeas corpus at least
Men plant mice nibble;
Without order, *cymrodyr*, in words
Become the underworld of weeds
Small crimes mount up. As
Media mince meaning out
Of words, marauding mice
Munch up the seed corn
And society starves.

We need symbols somewhere
Even sticks on little scaffold
On a sacred mound say
A mini-gibbet to fit a mouse.

# 'COUSIN SWIFT YOU WILL NEVER BE A POET'

*Dryden to Swift*

Who made you a poet?
The scrawl of the creeper on the outhouse wall
Is evidence but not the answer.

You picked it up like a child
Playing by ear and still unable to read
The tune that arrived
Like a swallow separated
From a mass migration

Of printed matter, a torn leaf
Caught in the hedgerow, messages in code
Wrapped around the ploughman's lunch

And soaking into the headland
Seeds and words nudging the furrow

In a snail's race
Towards canticles of fruition.

# JOB CREATION

Do you resent the solitude that is necessary
For creating new work?

Yes I do.

If you were tossed into a cyclonic whirl
And the dancing swept you up
So that your toes left the ground
And there was no space undisturbed
No cavity for creation
Would you resent that?

Yes I would.

What kind of conditions do you require?
Specify.

Alternating rhythms, ebb and flow.

Ah, advance and retreat.
Withdrawal and return.

Yes, those would be the conditions.

We have just the thing for you. Here
The playing card. Either Or,
Whichever way it falls.
Death in Life or Life in Death.

A neat design
And valid for the duration
Wet or fine
Just sign
Along the dotted line.

But ...

No buts. Next please.

# STEEL

Man who made steel has bent
Will and bone to grow
Arms that can couch the state
Ice that can stem the flow

Of blood of spoken words.
A sword that swings destroys
Boys and escaping birds.

The caterpillar tracks
Have marked the fallen walls.

I want to belong and it pains me to think
There's nowhere I fit in. Free critical mind
Is all very well. The cities where I practise my
Expertise are too big and of course I know I
Am too small, a mere face in the crowd all of us
Nobodies who yearn to be somebody. Once
In the *capella* above Gradoli I discovered
Under the dirt a genuine Messaro. I thought
I could settle here. Marta whom I met in Viterbo
Restoring Etruscan pots was locally born
A vital word 'local'. She had the Etruscan smile
I bought a ruined tower with a bit of land
And restored it. We adored the view. The lake
Drenched in history, shards of Etruscan domestic life
Still washed up on the black volcanic sand
The sunlight to cherish and the electric storms
Acceptable in our stone tower. Marta, bless her, Marta
Was the trouble. In Gradoli it seems over nothing
The butcher's wife turned on her and said she was living with
A foreigner, a rich German with more money than sense
And in an instant a wall went up as thick
As the one in Berlin. How could we settle?
We moved on. In Antibes Marta left me, I have
This fourth floor flat in Rue des Fleurs and the sun shines
Most of the time. But I don't belong here.

# TRANSPARENCE

The man made
Of glass do you
See through him
Or see yourself
Reflected in his gaze

His youth has gone
Before him so has
Your years spent
Polishing windows
Peering and seeing
Perhaps less than more.

In the first bloom
The flower reflects
Creation clarity
Reigns laughter
Wriggles like
A chrysalis.

The Dawn is flushed
With an understanding
That diminishes as
Knowledge accumulates
And the burden bends.

Nothing on the page as yet
And there may never be
Only her smile confirms
Love is solid

Empty the house
With the echo of
Stallions dancing
On the cobbled street

Hang her open window
On infinity
Her winged pen
Hovers above pearls

Satin stars
Nest
In her hair

And through her stare
Generations glide
In and out of
Embraceable silence.

# LOVE SONG

He was a small mass
Secreted at the heart of her industry

Around him
She invented an ordered flowering
Blooms hung like houses

Bees came and went
All afternoon
From the sharp sunlight through
Those easy portals

Petals grew
From the energy in her blood
Buds broke like dimples

Walls thick with custom
Gathered light
Plants bent towards her
And became her flowers.

Like a cat
The small man
Slept under the tree

But his shallow breathing enough
To shift his paper prayer wheel
In her direction.

# SILENCE

The geometry of silence
Inside symbols somewhere
But well out of reach
A pyramid perhaps sides
Smoother than marble
Not black only transparent colour
Trapped enraptured ecstasy
Without a mouth and yet
Somehow singing.

# CIVIL UNREST

It was a time of civil unrest of rumours
Ultimatums by word of mouth and the girl
Quite obviously had nowhere to go, adrift
Like an unenfranchised nationality
Without documents, displaced, clasping
Her fate with both hands like a valise with a broken lock
I was there to protect her a faceless shadow
And hear her mutter his praises. Her heroic Arthur
The talisman like an advert for
An unassailable product; she was too tired
To learn new catchwords while the old
Nostrums tumbled out like the teeth
Of the tattered comb in her hair.
She was on her own even though I
Was alongside her without a brush or comb
How could she keep her long hair in order
Mind you, the image I yearned for was a spotless virgin
A traditional damsel not a dirty
Refugee dragging her boots along
A filthy pavement

The true hero is tortured by the desire
To help. In fact or in fiction, he finds
It repulsive to leave a female, old or young,
Beautiful or ugly, dying on the roadside
Becoming a nameless corpse but alas
As they used to say, a shadow fearless or not
Is born without fingers.

The walls are covered with slogans, invitations
To excursions with planning permission
For untaxed holiday homes cool
Condominiums in hot climates and in the
Other world suburbs dripping with promises
And sweet memories peeling off the walls

The furniture hasn't arrived yet. Only
Leather bound volumes to sit on not to read
The walls plastered with legends and the stairs
Made of crystal able to bear the weight
Of shadows. The girl evokes Arthur
And he was there at least with iron hand
Ready to lead her into his cave

Where, contrary to all expectation
She found the place warm with
Bourgeois furniture and every corner
Spotlit. Now he said let the play
Begin not the nightmare.

Here history is reduced to a video tape
To be viewed with subtitles in every
Known language and all the more lurid
Mistakes of the human race recorded.
As unthreatening as music.
In fact I sing the tenor role myself. Tearful
Anthems. I keep the pubic hairs

Of prima donnas in a silver box like
Cherished keepsakes and if you wait long enough
You yourself can take a turn at
The well known tune.

The delight of history is love's embrace
Even though
The dear departed never sees
The heap of cut flowers withering on her grave.

# BATTLEFIELD

In that one wood
When the war was ending
The young man stood
In the early morning
And saw me walking
Without his head
And in the third wave
The boy still calling
While his entrails hung
Above the mud.

In that one wood
Two hundred lay dead
Who earlier drank
In a water-logged trench
And it had to happen
Between one and three
On a certain morning.

Later much later
He would sit up sweating
In bed at night
And hear Tom calling
The earth itself parting
In sudden fright.

For a thousand yards
In that one wood
The world lay dying
And nineteen years
Were nineteen stones.

# A CLERGYMAN MUSES

In most respects I was wrong
Oftener than I was right

Is this a condition we
Have to put up with or is it
A test?

Both.

Fail cheerfully on both counts
And keep going on wafers
Of optimistic conjecture.

God likes disgruntled servants.
How can you tell?
He gave this one three score years and ten
So that he could listen to
The music of my complaining

That's what rivers do
And the earth is full of rivers
Transforming the ugly clouds
Into glistening ripples
Where silver fish can swim
And moorhens dodge
Among the pencilled reeds

This is not a church
I wish to serve
Or the congregation
I would choose to study
With affection.

That is not the point.
Embrace their bad taste
And transform their shortcomings
Into an elegant suit
Of sackcloth and ashes.

# POUGHKEEPSIE

Embrace or analyse the fact.
His great grandfather came from Wales
And etched his name in slow letters
On the title page of his ornamental Bible
Under the red print 'Parch Peter Williams'
Which is more than the great grandson
In Poughkeepsie is able to read mark and inwardly digest.

He asked me what was it worth
This chunky volume with its brass clasp
In a new world which puts a price on anything
Even water and fresh air.

'*Gwerth y byd*' I said to him
Innocent creature with face and belly
Gleaming with prosperity and cheerful ignorance.
Then I remembered with the chill of guilt
A college principal's wife in Wales offering
An experimental painter from London a heap of Welsh Bibles
To be torn and scorched, drenched in colour
And glued up for ever, dead lips on a wall.

As the great grandson was readier to take my word
Than I was myself. How much for
Clogwyn Ddu'r Arddu, the raven's croak,
Windows red in the setting sun, the distance
Between the stirrup and the dust the instant
Williams called salvation.

Maybe all we have left to do is

Excavate the evidence and sell it like soap

To the fifth generation, or the fifth monarchy

If it matters at all

That a fragment of Welshness gathers dust in Poughkeepsie

This too is part of the mystery of being.

# BIRD ON A TWIG

Caught in the exigencies of seconds
He steps out surprising from his new Mercedes
Shining metal is armour plating
Against the petty invisibles the invisible worm
Draws on that papery skin

Compressed between ancestors and descendants
He reaches out a free hand
With the engine under his foot the world
Is an available system songs and stories
Await to refresh

He talks about the heart but it was his hands
Gloved in blood that struggled to revive it
The day was planted in its sunlight
One robin balanced on a rose tree twig
In greeting and farewell.

Type this and understand it. There are
Intermediaries less elusive than words
Languages that need not vanish
Visitations that never cross the threshold
And never leave. Let us call it
A presence and the promise of a presence
An unextravagant cadenza that occurs
While the moment waits flowing
Through syllables filling
The scientific measurement of seconds
With particles of light with operatic names
Like shadows shifting on the waters of the lake
This year or the year the war ended.
Doubt and certainty entertain
The same shadow that exists
In the same uncertainty
Whether present or absent
Dead or living.

# A DAY IN HAND

Awake! There are so few.
This bright coinage is
Going out of circulation
And no promise to
Replace them. Resort
To *y fynwent* where
Food and drink are not required.

# MANAWYDAN

Let us be clear about this, '*gymrodyr*'
It's a gallows not a trap
Made to fit a criminal not
The crime which was when all is said and done
Heinous – eating the seed corn of
A society going hungry
I am the judge and the hangman
I do my own dirty work I resist
The pleading in those nervous
Luminous eyes.

This is not myth, not
Metaphysical but
Physical enough and it won't
Be beneath my dignity to string up a mouse
And I won't be bribed.

However big the offer
The law which is there to
Protect us must take its course.

On the other hand I'm open
To plea bargain as far as
The rules allow.

I've got a sneaking feeling
There's more to this mouse
Than meets the eye.

The pulse could be
The delicate fluctuations
Of a lady's comely
Corset.

And the barely audible
Squeak the cry for help
Of a maiden in distress.

So what about it?

Release my lonely
And impetuous mother
From your master's spell

And her young paramour
If she demands it

And I will release
You
And restore you
To those who love you best.

The law and love
Can always come to an understanding
With the sting of compromise
A binding agreement.

# THE PEASANT

Poetry pinned him like a pelt
Against the barn door
Perception poured in sunlight
Over wood and skin.
This was the world
Of pain and pleasure
To contain all that
He wished to live in.

# A DOG'S LIFE

I am Cymro
Born of this place
Voice me

The shape of this island
Belongs to my feet
Review this situation
Not a private vision
No rock to stand on.

This is a narrow subject
No room for gestures
No corridors
Except into a tomb.

I am occupied
'For sale' hangs on my chest
My inheritance
Spilt into a car boot sale.

# TO THE SEA IN A SIEVE

Being vague is a way of life.
No one denies the shape of the city.
The map confirm it: nevertheless
Being lost is the preferred condition.

There is no greater deception
Than our passion for regulation.
Truth never nibbles: even the stars
Only presume the accuracy of their courses
Swim as we must in a sea
That can only be a sieve
And leads nowhere not even down.

Cutting down the Sacred Tree
Let it blossom again
Tribe or talent, they all protect
The stories of their people, in the
Conviction that by protecting the stories
They secure not only the past
But the future too.

# THE COURTEOUS DIG

Ah yes we all Ah yes we all
Long to be good and long to be tall
So passionately and then we fall
For dreams are thin and longings pall.

Into the train the white fox hopped
His jaws as wide as night
Five weak and wicked passengers
Were swallowed in one bite.

The epigram is not for me
Long wind demands long form you see
The epic is my cup of tea.

This is the position of the modern writer
The mooching of the itching shins
The glance that dusts a shelf of books
The pen that sketches eyes and brooks
Square circles signatures and keys
The buttocks that are hard to please
The cigarette that must be lit
The joke that makes it hard to sit
Until my wife has heard of it,
The multitude of infant sins,
This is where the work begins.

I hear the busy people
Consider me a drone.
'What does he do?' they mutter
In that worried undertone.

'Does he spend it
Like a butterfly
His overdraft on time?
Does he point the broom
And court the bee
With his heresies of rhyme?'

Shall I tell them there is profit
Compound interest in the hour
When the tremor of existence
Is fed by an imposing power

That can shift the gravestones
Like the tide a pebbled shore
And bring the dead to life again
And let the music soar

Bold with a better future
Where harpists play again
With intervals of music
To still our present pain.

# NOSTALGIA

Nostalgia for a well turned narrative
A story suspended in prose like
A fountain playing in the sunlight.
Talking to yourself isn't good enough
Or over-ripe recollections of
Sadness under an Indian summer.

Let men sweat with indecision
Inside their city suits
And politicians conjure new
Methods of betrayal
Take a subdued inventory
Of adulterous mire.

# THE DAMNED

Calling over the castle wall into the dark town
The Boy cried in the darkness of years before me
In the confusion of quoted days the accumulation
Of shared and lonely fragments, out of the thousand faces
That fly in the dark, who are the damned?

Borne by the spirit to the windy tower
He was given eyes to catalogue the lusty
Legion, they were taken in the act.

The lecherous bus conductor pushing
With finger the thigh of the standing blonde:
The white-haired ladies cheek to cheek
Pouring dirt down each other's ears, the agent
Bursting to tell his swindle spilling his beer
The big policeman, bald, pot-bellied, single
Soured, peeping at lovers on his evening beat

The bank clerk burning with envy of his school mates
New salary and new suit, the minister trading
His rubber conscience for the clapping hands
The teacher twisting the ears of the unattractive
And stupid Maggie, the boy burning
His brother's diary marked private, the farmer
Slitting the throat of the bag of precious wheat.

The damned the damned are indistinguishable
And crawl the earth like ants, blood is the fuel

Of evil, the boy cried, Evil is in the heart
My heart is in hell no heaven can pluck it out

Running he screamed upon the castle wall
His fingers tearing the wind, plucking the net of solitude
He flings his body from the wall of life.

The world is not an arena
Embrace me
Ancient muse
But not too close.

Empathy is not so easy
Words are as delicate as grass
You bend the stem
You study the seed heads
The broken joints
And hope also to be harvested.

Obligations are awesome
You can't live like swifts
In the summer heat
Harnessing the trees and the river.

You have to make a stand
Protect me
From the spinning earth
Lift your forgetful arms
To catch me
As the centuries grind me
To less than dust.

To be disinherited
Protect me
We entered this strange country

And the priest in the empty church
Spilt holy water
On my empty head.

# A MOTH AT ST JAMES'S

Dear little insect
That's what they called you, Mosca, I can't think why,
This evening almost in the dark.
As I was reading Deuterisiah
You reappeared alongside me
But without your spectacles
So you couldn't see me
And at first I couldn't recognise you
Without their glitter in the haze.

No specs no antennae
Poor insect with wings
That only spread in the imagination
A pretty tattered bible, not much
To be relied on, the black of night
A flash of lightning a rumble of thunder
And then no storm. It can't be
You left so quickly without a word?
But it's too absurd to think
You still had life.

At the St James in Paris I'll be obliged
To book a single (They don't relish
One-off single guests) And the same I suppose
In the phoney Byzantine where you stay
In Venice: then right away discover
The cubby hole of the telephone girls
Always your good friends: take leave

Again before the battery needs recharging
The urge to have you with me again
Let it be no more than a gesture or habit

We used to practise for the Hereafter
A whistle a sign of recognition.
I'm trying now to moderate it with a hope
That we are all of us already dead without knowing it.

# BROTHERHOOD

Other poets
Are not opponents
So do not be
Encouraged comrade
By their deficiencies
The juice of
Creativity they tell me
Is universal brotherhood.

# JACOB'S COAT

A blue moment
Is a votive urge towards
Eternity trapped
In an iambic flame

Until other rhythms
Flow in and only the canvas
Space you used to call it

Calling to the heart
Of a coloured cosmos

Call it what you like
Or will words as such
Don't matter.

Even music is silent
Caught in an interval
Where joy and terror
Transfix each other and blood
Becomes the source of
Jacob's colours.

# THE DEAD

*adapted from 'Y Meirwon' by Gwenallt*

You can see clearly enough when you pass middle age
Those people that place that made you what you are
Graves in two graveyards in Allt Wen
Are ropes of steel that grip more tightly than rage.

When I rode those bits of bikes pinched from the scrap heap
And played rugby for Wales with inflated pig bladders
I had no idea two of my pals in the team
Would leave their lungs a red spew in battered buckets.

In the terrace our next-door neighbours hailed from Merthyr Tydfil
The martyrs we called them not the Merthyrs
Their coughs, five of them in turn shot across the wall
And put a stop to our laughter and kept us listening still.

We slipped into the bible parlour to stare with surprise
At flesh like charcoal in the coffin and at ashen voices.
It was there above lids screwed down before their time
We learnt our red rubrics and made rebellious choices.

Not respectable death that jingles his keys
Like a warder making the rounds of his cells
But a mechanised beast who leaps in the dark
Or lurks in the furnace to kill a man as he works.

The hooter's knell: death drunk with dust and smoke
Death dressed like a destiny of blue fire
Or flooding pits and forcing us to barbaric despair
As we fight with catastrophic powers to throw off the yoke.

# WISE MAN

The wise man does not fear what comes
Beyond the ditch of death
What gives him pause is life itself
The nightmare drawing breath.

Mild manners get you nowhere.
Get your teeth stuck in, learn to
Suffer and inflict suffering. The ceremonies
Of spring are decorative deceptions
God and his wisdom lie in
The appetite and the devouring blood.

As for lyrics print sharper discords. Grind
Unspeakable melodies from groans
Visit for the first and last time
The shunting trains with their cargo
The *Dies Irae* of the world's despair.

Soft prayers are only there
To suffocate imprecations
Victims are entitled to
Elaborate curses. Weave weave

A spider's web to trap
The smiling apple and transform
Any stupid joy into a
Grinning skull and broken heart.

If the meaning of life is terror
What's wrong with being frightened?
Whose imagination conjured up a pack
Of vampires at the door?
Why bother
Aren't there enough humans around
Or vampires at the door. Blood
Has a sweeter purpose. Measured
Action comes with thought. Evil
Is a miasma of the mind. Nobody
In their right senses – where do they keep
Them – nobody innocent as a horse
Can order a holocaust
Keep your knees in order – any day
In the new millennium a chastened god
Will mount the altar in Athens
And by transporting in the internet
Of power to Washington
Built out of blood.

# SUNDAY SCHOOL

I was taught in Sunday School
That 'love thy neighbour'
Had political implications
And I took the meaning to heart.
There was only one slight snag
My neighbour was unaware I existed.

# THE HOUSE HUSBAND

She asked me down for the weekend. What else
Could I do? Work was slack. I felt redundant
An architect with nothing to build so
I agreed and drove all the way down there
Into the depths of another country
To regret it.

Until one of the crew piped up
At breakfast that wet Sunday morning
'Do you know something,' he said 'We are sitting
Less than ten miles from the mouth of hell.'

This amused her. Queen of all
She surveyed in the hotel breakfast room
Exercising unobtrusive authority
Over a dozen men well paid
To produce specific quantities
Of candy floss and tinsel.

He was a native.
And even here my wife Adele was on the lookout
For what she called potential: not rape
And pillage and slaughter every time but enough
Spectacular spread to keep the public
Happy: not bread and circuses she said
More salami slices of the same spiced
Ingredients to shaft the opposition and shake up the schedules
I'm not trying to say she's cynical. Just a woman

Who knows her business; bright images
Sharp sensations and dialogue so spare and taut
That she would snap it between her elegant fingers

And plots of course. With twists. The familiar
Made unfamiliar. Her job was on the line
As she explained to herself as she lay in bed
'Executives carry the can. Put not your trust
In heads of department or princes and never
Commit yourself to dodgy film directors
However charming. And above all mind your back
And keep a close eye on the ratings'
I murmured sympathy and dangled
The 'do not disturb' sign on the door-knob
For all the good it did me.

This focus puller or whatever he was
Had a peculiar name; Pryderi or some such.
He always looked flushed as though he'd been drinking
Even first thing in the morning. Adele
Licensed a listen. At least, her expression
Said, it was preferable to staring
Through a wet window at the weather.
It might take her mind off budget margins
Abandoned set-ups, re-shoots
Career moves in her absence
Departmental treacheries ...

'Not so much the Mouth of Hell. Call it the gateway
To the other world. There's a prince involved,
And a Shadow King, and not a film crew in sight
Only two packs of hounds.'

He forged on in spite of frivolous comment,
He had my wife's approval and hers was the last word,
He also had a raucous baritone
That could ride the noise and arrive
At a respectful silence. He spoke

As if every every phrase he used had a double
Meaning it bounced out of one language
Into another. He was small and strange
Good at his job, Adele said, and she told me she had
To restrain herself from calling him a hobgoblin
'Hey hobgoblin come to heel'

'The hind was bleeding at his feet you see
And his hounds were where they had no business to be
Like selfishness itself tearing innocence
Apart, muzzling the blood and torn flesh
With the ferocity of untamed desire'

Ironic applause from his colleagues
For his eloquence: but he topped it all
With an explosive self deprecating chuckle

'You bunch of ignorant metropolitan buggers!
I shan't detain you with anthropological detail
I wouldn't want to embarrass you
With the wealth of my scholarship and the
Amplitude of my inherited knowledge
Of fertility myths and cosmic curiosities
Connected to the seasons and the way corn
Springs from the blood of disobedient sons.

Not that *he* disobeyed. No, he indulged
His hunting instinct at the expense of his honour.
I don't expect you freebooting scabs
To understand that. Take my word for it
The beauty of the earth can never transcend
The indolence of men. Why stop to look at a tree
While your enemy lurks behind it
Aching to kill you. And may all this
Be a lesson to all you ignorant bastards
Blundering about down here fiddling your expenses
With your tongues hanging out like greedy dogs
In waiting to take advantage of our women.'

'Pryd,' Adele said Her voice of authority
Woven in silk, 'Get on with the story'

'Adele! My darling! Anything for you
But don't you think I missed my vocation?
Be that as it may, you rude mechanicals,

At the mouth of hell the truth will out
It is the only passport.'

'What's a hero?' He stood up
Short and stumpy and pointed at himself
'Not me, you need a man who can touch
The pulse of being, Prepared to reverse
The seasons. I sing of the King my father
Who saw himself in a mirror of reproach
And offered his life in recompense
For a moment's misdemeanour.'

'Pryd' Adele said 'Spell it out
In words of one syllable, enlighten us'
She waved her cigarette and in that moment
The director who I reckoned was the source
And origin of Adele's disquiet sidled
Like a snake into the vacant seat by her side
Offering to light her cigarette. 'Adele'
I heard him whisper 'Could I have a word?'
I savoured her cool response I saw
Him swallow his masculine pride
And I rejoiced. There he sat, Franco,
The latest flavour in television chic
With his so-called Hollywood connections
Exposed in an inadequacy somehow
Greater than mine. And there was our Adele
Giving the focus puller his signal
To continue in his boisterous mode.

'What you morons need to understand
The only discipline that counts for a leader
In our Byzantine world is self-discipline.
For example one blow may resolve a quarrel
But a second merely renews it. And so on
Over and above that if we aspire
To control the seasons, comrades, we can only
Do so in reverent alliance with a god.
This means obedience and self discipline.
It would be for this he would like the place
Of a lord of the underworld at the ford
And destroy the enemy with that single blow
So that the world of nature could continue
As a source of perpetual refreshment.'

Ironic interruptions 'Do we
Have a plot here?' Franco trying
To salvage his self-esteem by sounding
One of the boys 'Case and catastrophes' he said
'They grab the ratings, Pryd, and don't forget
They keep you out of the dole queue'
Adele hadn't smiled. His ribaldry
Petered out. Pryderi's voice grew louder

'A hero must sublimate his aggression
So that disobedience can be transformed
By a punishment that is also
A reward. Do you follow me?'

'Blindly', Adele said. The rest guffawed
Like a class of rowdy children. I listened
As though it might be a message meant for me.

'The shadow king rehearsed his sacrifice,
"I will put you in Annwn in my place
So that no one who ever followed me
Shall know I myself am not you
Not even my wife. One year and a day
Comes the encounter between me and our enemy
At the ford. You will stand there in my stead
And the one stroke you strike he shall
Not survive and when he begs to be dispatched
With yet another you refuse however much
He pleads or he will revive to fight again
And restore the threat of desolation."

'He exchanged his shape with the king
Of the underworld. For a year and a day
He governed the court, kept enemies at bay
And as part of the covenant
Slept with the king's wife'

'Ah ha!' said Franco. 'Surely something here for us?
Sleeping with the king's wife. A fresh twist
To tweak the ratings round about week
Thirteen?' A bid for Adele's approval
Crushed like a cigarette butt in her saucer.

Pryderi's voice grew more powerful
As he cupped his hand over his right ear.
' "When a true prince lives in his place
He commands a double kingdom!" In triumph
They met again at the mouth of hell, exchanging shapes,
And the shadow king repossessed his court
With a secret joy partaking of customs
And courtesies with friends and retainers
All unaware of his long absence

'And when it was time to quit the feast
The king made ready for bed and his wife
Came to him. He spoke to her with renewed
Affection and surrendered himself
To the pleasure of love. Now this
Was something she had not been used to
For a whole year and the thought
Grew in her mind '"Lord god
Why should it be different this night
From what it has been this past year?"
She wondered so much that when
He spoke to her a second time and even a third
He got no answer "Why are you silent?
Will you not speak to me?" "I shall tell you"
She said "Because for one whole year
I have not spoken this much in this bed"
"How can you say so when you have been
As deeply intimate as ever this night?"

"Let it be my shame if it must, my lord,
For a whole year since from the moment
The bedclothes covered these bodies
There has been neither pleasure nor talk
Between us nor have you ever turned
Your face towards me"

'Then it was his turn for thought "O Lord
God, such a steadfast prince and such
Unswerving friendship have I found
In that strange encounter. The ferocity of the world
Can be tamed by the calendar of grace"
"Lady" he spoke out loud "I am to blame and
Not to blame. Hear me" And he told
Her the full account so that she too
Might testify before God that her husband
Had found an incomparable companion.
So strong in faith to withstand
The continuing temptation of the flesh.'

Adele was smiling 'Why don't you two
Nip off and find the mouth of hell? You shouldn't
Have too much difficulty in finding it.
You know something, Pryd? In a society
Fed on scandal, chastity is as
Marketable as mildewed bread.'

The focus puller looked swollen by his story.
His authority would challenge hers

'Love must be sanctioned. Not secret.
That's one point. The other must be that
Chastity is a state of the heart of
Civilised existence and if that is
The case ...' Adele became impatient

'How do you shoot it? That's a funny old problem,
Can't you cook up something original
Identical twins for instance one sweet
As apple pie the other evil that sort of thing
With lashings of mayhem thrown in
Slashing bruise-bloody bathrooms
And cars like bullets screaming
Through the moonlit streets,
And where's the woman's angle?'

Franco whispered in her ear 'Adele
Could you spare me twenty-four hours?
London. There and back. Something I need to fix'
I saw no trace of intimacy in his smile
The boyish appeal, the promise. Adele
Was like ice – 'Take all the time you like'
She said, 'You've been replaced.'

He got his word in before he left
At the wheel of his BMW. 'Mind your back
Old man,' he said, 'House husbands
Are easier to replace than good directors
See you around when you get back
To the underworld. Meanwhile have a nice day.'

The sinners, said Satan
I'll take them all. I have
Ample accommodation
Poor wretches. They are so
Easily persuaded. Even
When the flames shoot up
They clap their hands
At last they cry
The great fair
Has come.

# MAKING BUTTER – OLD STYLE

*De Senectute (Cicero)*

Age as you bend me
Into the last turn
With my head in my hands
Let me spin in the churn.

The axle is oiled
By the music of time
The calendar ruled
By the tyrant rhyme.

Each to his own
In the box of sighs
The sky is painted
A window of lies.

Love is the handle
My ancestor said
The vessel still turns
But they are all dead.

Who eats the butter?
Who bakes the bread?
The kings of heaven
My ancestor said

But he's obsolete now
At rest in St Fagans

They carried him there
On a horse drawn wagon.

And use my old hymn book
To steady the churn
Folk pay to watch working
With cool unconcern

As if earth had no axis
No handle no oil
And the flat earth a plateau
Of sterilised soil.

# THE ART OF WAR

The messages of earthly peace
Are woolier than unwashed sheep
Lifting an eye to skylarked skies
Converting bleats to anguished cries

The proponents of the art of war
Are smartly dressed and wholesome
They do not reek of human blood
Or corpses rotting in the mud.

Machines need victims so propagate
The human race from pole to pole. At heaven's gate
Exterminations operate
The gates are shut. Outside the suicidal swarms
Feed the celestial sewage farms

O who can save the human race
From cutting its nose to spite its face
Send for the scholars by the truck
And have them shovel up the muck.

Childhood friends who leave to die
In far off countries
Converse in the setting sun
Like shepherds among olive trees

All their flocks have given up grazing
Their bells are silent and the slow
Mist rises around their wool.

The swineherd from the underworld
Emerges between the trees
His herd black obedient and smooth
Silent at his heel.

In the dusk the gestures of their conversation
Grow mountains, create
Another horizon, wavering blue lines
That conjure the cloak of night
To hide childhood friends.

This is their territory
The Hesperides do not need
Tourists at tables.
Send the blue coat of night
As the white flocks give up grazing
And their bells are silent.

# THE COLONEL'S WIFE

An armed man
Decorated for slaughter
His boots
I lick
They aspired
To rank
They arrived
He was first to the ridge
His eye blown out
He turned and hollered
Where the hell you bin?

I married that man
I saw through his eyes
Parachutes on steeples
A headless boy
A boot filling with blood
The smell of Death
Hidden in the hedges.

I call him honey
He touches me
Like the sound of music
He has come through

At night
When I count the stars
This criminal sweats

In my arms
The teddy bear
Under his pillow
Cries in his sleep.

How can you blame the architects
The church employed them
To encapsulate the glory of God
Not extend it
No blood on the stones
The sacrifice was organised
The rewards equitable
And the mystery?
More absent than ever
To the people below.
A transubstantiation
Into a host of vessels.

Interest accumulated: in the bathroom
Each morning he considered his wealth
And to ease his soul
He shot metaphors.

# MONTALE CABINERA

He wrote that the blackcap wasn't shot
As far as he knew. Well here nobody shoots them.
They disappear all the same and the fact
Doesn't make news. From the point of view of the bird
Our staggering ignorance makes sense
Because it is as unattractive and more random than our weather.
Consider the *mise en scène*: brambles, rose briers, evergreen shrubs
And pan-handled rhododendrons like superfluous arguments
Straggling over a hillside. They are there to signal our absence
We attach ourselves like insects to the vegetation
To hide and breed to copulate and die
And all our flights are short and jerky.
Our phantoms have as much substance
As our presence and that's why bishops like birds
Have wings.

# SURVIVAL

In my narrow mindset
The solar-system
Is a model of restraint.

The size of planets
Corresponds to capsules
Of human passions.

Cosmic love spins on an even
Axis beyond the razor
Winds of hatred and revenge.

In which case why
Are the ferocious antics
Of soldier ants
And humankind
So threatening?

Only because
I lie trapped
Inside this shivering self
Determined to survive.

# THE BOAT

The boat broader
Than a bed drifting
Towards a continent poised
As the earth is between
Sovereign spaces.
There was an hotel enlarging with importance
And an iron desert manned
The promenade nobody could invade.
Far beyond there was a forest
Evergreen and frozen with voices
Hoarse and timeless teeming with
Information and learning nothing
To learn the boat rocked
In pleasing silence.

# MORE

*i*

Trapped without his frame
The room became an ocean
And life a sequence of islands
He could see but no longer
Reach. She was the principal
Inhabitant. There must have been
Others. From each direction
She bent towards him that
Ingenious smile that wore
Love as fleeting as a Life.

*ii*

First he sought to project himself
So deeply into others, he could speak
And even feel on their behalf. Then
He sought equilibrium, a calm
Absorbing colour a world
Of calm. Now he stares through
A thick window of indifference,
Can this be the calm he set out to find?

*iii*

It is not difficult to take aim
At characters you dislike. Pick
Out movements to show them at
Disadvantage. Deliver that unguarded word
With the false polish of a smile

Beware. In each unappealing
Portraitist is the sour features of your
Own character reflected.


*iv*

Ah what a Fate. Daily a hopeless ferment
Of unused words bombarded his small skull
As he crouches on his elbows
Composing headlines for the *Daily Liar*
An electric storm
Tears his cerebellum apart
With the vocabulary of another tongue
Distant voices invade his brain
Daily but never
Set him free, credo
Never paid off a mortgage.


*vii*

Here nobody holds me responsible
For anything. Not even myself. Is this
Delicious or demeaning? I have all day
To ponder questions, disinter
Slippery philosophical questions that
Lie breathless on an empty beach
While I mutter prayers at speed
Like savage incantations.

*viii*

Shall I shave today? Maybe
Maybe not. So much choice
Without that moral obligation
You used to insist upon. Choice
Government approved, the first step
Towards the celestial city; that
Consumers' paradise politicians promise
As to democratic rationing only
The over-eighties look back not
Forward. This choice is the beginning of
The end.

*ix*

While my hair kept growing and the seas
Salty busy maniacs disguised as
Statesmen exterminated people
To perfect some design or other
Cooked up in draughty garrets or
Public libraries by frustrated artists
Resolved to make the world pay
For the boils on their backsides
*Mens sana in corpore sano*. If only.
Beware sharp minds above decaying teeth.

*x*

Everything in the History
Of this world has been done

And done better; Therefore
Child of chance by all means
Look for the Roots, but
Don't eat them.

*xi*

The sober atheist, the Hamlet
Of our day, rejects the concept
Of an Afterlife: should it occur
Will he spurn the road
To a Celestial City and leap
Into a private Dark

*xii*

A civilised world prepares
Its own elegy, so that when
It comes the orchestra is ready
French horns sigh, strings shiver
As they make way for the row of
Drums, a muscular angel puts
The trumpet to his lips, the streets
Crack open, the living and the dead
Mingle and look up as
The dark skies announce
An agonising day of judgement.

We are doomed the priest said
So set about our destruction
If it must be better
We do it ourselves
Give me a mechanical
God, not a robot without
Appetite a worker god yearning
To be fed on sacrificial blood
And for me the sinecure
Of self-fulfilling prophecy.

I catch my poetry as sleep catches my eyelids.

A little sleep holds the music

And I walk well among the words

That are as erect as the petals of well-bred tulips,

As hard-working as children eating jam,

As friendly and as wilful as small quantities of cascading water

As little as larks, as long as a woman's love,

Until the clock rocks

And Time leaps in my lap.

Time stretched out
Is not a bridge
It is liquid
Along with the oracular
Dribble of old age
Fleeting thoughts exalted
Feelings sharp perceptions
Float like plankton
In an immeasurable ocean
Of consciousness

There may be other forms
Of life that feed on them
However they do not
Eat numbers.

Dates to which we cling
And long to keep
Offer no nourishment.
The rings on old trees
Can sigh in captivity
But not sing
Like your notes played on a page.

# WHISPERS

*i*

Whose history, she whispers
Does it matter. There was a second
The sun stood still. Your landscape
Emerged complete with mountains and
Its language. Briefly you were a heartland
Of power your own universe
Complete with constellations
And an earth that triumphed.

*ii*

Look we've never been this way before
And yet nothing seems different
Blue as ever rhymes with view
All the same, here each step is
An illumination. Love sent us here
Love does not change or put up
Directions his clock has no fingers
The moonlight will last until
We see a shape that whispers
You are back home.

*iii*

You should be sliding to oblivion
Instead you scramble on a scree of words
As if all that needs to be said had never been said
There you go like women on hands and knees sifting waste
While all the world is still low clouds and coal dust

You talk about late harvest and the sacred flame
Before you write words are washed away.

*iv*

The bird said I think they are technically perfect
As I stroked his feathers, Mind my beak
Most of us fly without thinking
Which is just as well or we'd
Fall out of the sky. Thought is
Dangerous and never went
With flight. And that is why
Our joy is unconfined as we
Glide the thermals. Smooth as a sigh.

*v*

Bedtime in a house scheduled for demolition
The windows already gone no story
Left to tell the floor littered
With a block of letters someone else
Can clear up into a bin or a book
Dreams of inconsequence sift
Through the dust and the incurious air.

*vi*

Coming to the end of it all her eyes
Shepherded the clouds beyond the bedroom window
They would have no idea where to go
Without her glance. On her lips

The shape of two words, *Ein Tad*,
Made to fit any language any age
Saints at this very corner had need of them
To keep the clouds on course.


*vii*

Drifting through the wayward waters
Of consciousness night and day
How can you tell what the familiar figures
Of the settlements on the shore mean
What they are saying, strange disturbing
Music speech is more than birdsong
But less than silence
The faint outline of a prayer.


*viii*

Ice cream on the kitchen floor
Sinful delight beyond the table leg
A kitten bigger than a cat
Exchanges stare for stare is it
Joy or Fear? The mistakes of a lifetime
Swim in the same beam of sunlight
A gentle hand smelling of an antiseptic
Extends a pot of soothing something
Within range of lips that
Need a wet-wipe as they mutter an
Expression that must mean 'thanks'.

Mortality is written

With bones

Not words

That have no use

For tenses unlike verbs

They dispose our fears

Our histories

Our illusions

Like iron filings

They exist inside

Their own fields of force

Seasons that come and go

Impress them, anonymity

And patience their

Music dark rhythms

Muffled drums

In Latin

Caesar's bones.

Broader than a bed the boat

Drifted towards a continent anchored

As the earth is inside the measured

Notes of space beyond the pale shoreline

A grand hotel empty bulged with

Importance above a smooth promenade

Where my feet were not tempted and felt no fear.

The way things can happen
Old men after the event tell you
'I told you so', soothsayers, fortune-tellers
In tents, politicians claim extra whatsits sensory perception, the
Knowledge cross their palms and count
The tealeaves; what invisible hand
Brought us together? A breath of solar
Wind, a sunspot an auspicious
Constellation? In such a moment
Lifetimes lurk the earth turned
As the poet said with stones and trees
And rivers and we flowed on to
This point of parting when one forges
Ahead into the open sea.

Better left unsaid? Virtually
Everything, at this point in time when
The actor pauses for effect we trust
Not just forgetting the crucial line
To be crossed into deeper understanding
Conscious as he may be poor devil
Of the expectations of a sea of frowning
Critical faces. Here he can seize the
Moment of unexpected triumph, turn
On his heel and smirk at the tyrants,
'The rest is silence'.

The brass bedstead they manoeuvred
So that the old man could see the world
Through the bedroom window, a bed
He said to be born in, not borne again
His white moustache twitching with a lifetime
Of good humour, the yellow nightcap he
Favoured more for effect than warmth tipping
Over his night eye. He saw Cae Canol
Bulge uphill grazed by sheep he disapproved of
And the thick hedge like a frontline bulging
With birds, nests and rabbit holes which he said
Was as it should be — God bless this hedge and all that
Lives in it. Such things they overheard whether
He intended or not. He sipped his soup under his
Moustache, smiled and muttered until the
Day he fell asleep and they could not wake him.

# THE GEESE OF TIME

The geese of time are marching out of Fairyland
In one straight line. As you say
They give no warning except to hiss
'So soon is soon' While we live the Milky Way
Is the only way to travel. Stay where you are
The legend will overtake you.
Just wave your inarticulate hand.

# PROVINCIAL SONG

When I'm stuck in Llanrwst
How I long for East Grinstead
The shopping arcade
The worn steps to the square
Voices of England where you know what they're saying.
One can't understand
And one doubts if it's worth it
What these people are saying
Or what makes them tick –
Ah vision of heaven, how I wish I was there.

The rain clouds gather
Above the grim mountains
I feel in my muscles
That tinge of despair
The way that they talk is designed to exclude me
It growls like a lion at the top of the stairs

I want to climb in
My legs are inclined to
Hail fellow well met
Is my motto for life
To be met with a scowl and a lack of acceptance
Makes me reach for my gun, not to mention my wife.

# RECIPE FOR A POET

The poet unlike the orator or worldly wise
Cannot belong to the world as he belongs to nature
That is to say he can't go thumping a tub or criticise
The Age like an anthropoid-sociologist expert on culture.
Because of his birth born of an inhuman
Unsympathetic witch who specialised
In introducing shooting stars and sunsets from her cooking pan.

The sins of the age like a preacher or an expert on industrial culture
All because of his birth born of an unsympathetic
Unredeemed witch obsessed with stars and sunsets.
Melting the sad and the healthy into one emetic
With her back turned on the world's shrinking outlets
Nevertheless when he finds the one right world a thunderbolt
Shall shake all our routines, make visible
Ghosts at the feast and phantoms on their way to the fair. One jolt
Is enough to make the universe feasible
And pushes the tribes towards the mosques or a mascot
As a flood snuffs out the sun.

# WHERE THEY ARE GONE

Where are they gone
That held the field
And taught an epoch
What to feel

I knew them as I know myself
At breakfast puzzled by the night
And shadows from another world
That took away their appetite

Fame made them glisten
Heard them talk
Like messengers from outer space
And what they said
Froze on a lake
And caused the winter wilderness

They left behind tall walls of stone
And terraces where children stumble
Windows that square up to the dark
Floors smooth like servants, meek and humble
But mere moments cannot satisfy
The lust to go beyond and grasp
The hands that aged at dining tables.

# A BLESSING

We are all descending
Into old age and death
Like skeletons with raincoats
On their arms. Thought
Which uses flesh
Has gone to seed
But out of this arid land
Of unconsciousness
A new world of colour
Will thrust forth the smiles
Of our successors.

# WEALTH

The governing classes
Embellish appropriate spaces
Their purpose to
Enlarge our
Limited perspectives.

To be photographed
In yachts
Is never self-indulgence
They love lots

Of charities
They patronise
So do not envy
Their privileged condition.

What they enjoy
They suffer you
To share
In coloured pictures.

Their elders their villas
When the wind tunes up
Before log fires
Forget the terrors of the street
And dream of
Riots easily subdued.

Of love and loyalty

Like marble

Petrified our idols

Half hidden by oleanders

Take in sightless sunset

Vast salt waters and porphyry rocks

Empires of salt water and obedience.

Don't rush when you read me
Between words as between lovers
There are hesitations that
Mean as much if not more
Than the coloured links
In the chain

    Singing is a better
Exercise: a note embraces
A note without invading
Its appropriate space. There's
Order then beyond arrangement
And light with the authority
Of successive dark.

Beware of the reissue he said
It suffocates perception, it
Smoothly encompasses a world
That's bigger than a prosody – that's what he said

    Not to mention
Parentheses asides refinements
Thinner than dissected tissue

    Don't expect
Me to sing melodic swerves
Glissandi equidistant thumps

They are not in my line
I embellish appropriate spaces
And thereby enlarge other people's
Perspectives as well as my own
Between me and my amanuensis
A divine afflatus hovers
Your function reader is to give respect.

Those details
That belonged to you
Are now transferred
To me
But in the process
They have lost
Their bright autonomy
Like flowers once cut
They cannot bloom
With a resplendent power
Life's deeper revelations
Live and die
Within the shrinking hour.

Prisons. Crematoria. Deserted Emmaus.
The skull conserves. White memory on
White walls. Words contain us
There is no escape. Why should there be?

Outside these walls colours
Of other worlds shift with the tides.

Herein comfort like fading love song
Flickers in the courtyard. Wardens are
Shadows, an eye in the forehead of every door
Full of promise and friendly punishment.

Whispers are fragile as bones cracking
And all those pardons offered, brochures
Of release from year to year
In return for lip serviced a full confession
Who controls the great feast and when it comes
Shall we be at or on the table?

Meanwhile the flight of a moth
Dust on the cold stone, flowers
Darkness, centuries woven in webs
Until the rainbow gives birth
And the column rambles through
Solitude to the edge of the last page.

Chance that has neither face
Nor hands yet sees
How we squeeze through the sour channel of remorse

Orders our disorder: breaks our chains
Preserves a balance of despair
Lowers the temperature spreads the disease
Transforms our helpless fields of force.

Chance has neither hands nor face
Only a will to set the pace
That daily keeps the stars in place
If this is true the human race
Is right to worship Providence
When all is done day becomes night
And hunger thrives on appetite.

# GODODDIN

Gilded with rank
Bold in the vanguard
Shy and breathless
Confronted by a woman
He paid in full
For the palace mead.

The round shield dented
With the cries of battle
In his frenzy
Mercy was frozen
He came to battle
In search of blood
In the ranks still standing
He flashed like a sickle
Reaping the reeds.

His actions are counted
When Gododdin sings
On the palace floor.

His followers live
His losses are light
Before Madoc's tent
One in a hundred.
He deserves praise.

The bollards in the piazza were not meant to be sat on
The wealthy facade of the terraces were never meant
As a partial embrace and still the world contains us
As one indefatigable dream: age has nibbled the edges
Mottled the skin and even the eyes, those startled eyes
Are sparkling with a dubious revelation.
Was it true what they felt or was it fiction
Neither the story table nor the critical intelligence
Control the translucent bubble that alone protects them both
From unceremonial extinction.

# THE SAG IN THE CLOTH

The house is acceptable
As it stands surrounds us
With warm walls familiar
Pictures pulsating their own shadows

Becomes alien when
Taken over by others tramps
Builders soldiers. Harsh
Thumps of tools and weapons
Shorten the day
And darken the night.

To be dated
Is not necessarily
Beware of adverbs
To be castrated.

Even as with clothes
Beware the sag in the cloth
Fashion is a wheel
Of variable size
A differential designed
To absorb transitions.

So be absorbed
As the academic
Who scrutinises

His colleagues' publications
For plagiarism.

Take nothing for granted
And date each paragraph
As it emerges
And reappears hours later

On the airport carousel
Where time is money
And standstill is collapse.

# HOLY ORDERS

*i*

God loves a disgruntled servant
How do you know? The Old Testament
Is stuffed with them.

In most respects then as now
They guessed wrong as often as
They guessed right. Nevertheless
We revere their authority
Because their growls
Are so well grounded
In our dumb misgivings.

The church is a stone
Rectangle surrounded
By savages with long knives.
The Rector in its pulpit
Shuts his eyes so tight
We know there can be
Nothing to be afraid of.

And we listen neutered
By the music of his complaint.

*ii*

O Lord this is not the nation
I longed to serve not
The congregation I would

107

Choose to look at with affection.
They doze indoors
On winter afternoons
And their faith
Seeps into the
Woodwork

While I learn
To forgive and chastise
In unequal measure.

# GIVING UP

As his head lowered friction
Grew out of proportion, not his own
But flashed vivid with other narratives
Wicked man, innocent children in black hats
Domestic women in antique clothing
All the ages congealed into a tired head.
We argue perhaps with cold efforts of creation
And too weak to resist another spring
A green revolution and the old call to action.

All that afternoon I lived
In the nineteen thirties and never
Felt them tremble under my feet.
November, another winter would approach
Poppies and monuments remind
The Great War behind us. True
My father, after being gassed was given eggnog to drink
Between lessons the playground was surrounded
By chestnut trees and conkers abounded
Eddie Evans and I sat on the school wall
Recording motor cars as they went by
Six three to me as more models motored
West than East, if only I could spell
Their names as well as their numbers
Armstrong Siddeley, Alfa Romeo, Lee Francis.
Those were the days. The Twilight lingers
And nights drive you to bed. That world
That twixt and between. The timeless emblem of the earth
As children fell asleep.

Like a poem?
What pretension
You must allow it
Since she looked
At the world through
The loving lens of old age.

She saw a war
Of angels between
The affections and folly.

# MAKING A DIFFERENCE

Had you written then
What you know now
Would it have made a difference?

That sweet face hid a stern lady
Not the rose
Not the lily
And none of the attitudes
Of innocence that shone
Only in your pen
Never in your eyes.

Books that bend
Corners of history
Perish
Genes that send
Qualities to cherish
Vanish like any mystery.

Don't leave me
Death
The stern lady
Sits on the bed
The innocence
shines
In both her eyes
The coldness
Is in her hands.

All is the same
From a distance
Sadness mirth
Melt praise and blame
Die in the same instant.

Aware of being aware
The days advance with the remorseless unheeding
Unstoppable accuracy of library stamps
Even writing your name
Is a political form of depression.
How to address your raised
Feathered hat.
How did he pass the time
Encumbered with so much intelligence
Dozing on the alpine terrace
Equating himself with the peaks
White and perfect and the people
Like the dog at his feet
Allowed to lick his limp hand
As he schemed in the sunlight
And waited for the ripe hour
At which to strike.

# DICTATOR

Let's take this thing backwards
And in character
This morning I felt I could knock holes in the universe
And memory was nowhere
If the race was in trouble
The human race not just one colour
I would take it over
Reconstruct creation
Without smashing it to bits
Reaching out to the corners of the falling houses
And holding up the walls
Anticipating wounds and bending rifles
Dispatching bombs down those very holes
And building instead of hangers and silos
Impossible Halls, Mansions of Perfection.

Now in the night
The tremor of memory reasserts its own control
The old dictator stalks as he always did
In a hub of evil dispatching cattle trucks
To rattle through the sleeping suburbs
Nothing he says is new
Yet the fear is fresh as dew.

I suffered in his hands for generations
Failure is his desert
His word the capsule of a living death.

Rebel! Revolutionary devotee
Of the rights of man. What protection we ask
Does your manifesto afford
As we lie naked white between
Black jackboots and a loaded
Automatic pointed at your ear?

Does this seem to be the beginning
As you retire from the living world
Will we ever know?

In that first winter
When the war was won
We travelled homeward
Watched the setting sun
So much unfinished
So much not begun.

They appear before their people like plastic gods
When they dance
The stamp of their egos
Makes the earth quake

What people swallow is
Sugared poison
To still believe
He was a farm boy
And she washed dishes

Why is the truth so salty?
The news will come when
You least need it
And the prison door is firmly shut.

# FREEDOM

That afternoon I took a Jeep
And drove through the Tuscan
Vineyard to the mountain lake.
Why did I never learn to swim?
I was trapped there in the dust
All those busy years ago.

# HEN GERDD

A man's strength

The body of a boy
Ready for the slaughter
All those stallions
Subdued
By his bright thighs
His smart shield dangles
Over their tamed quarters
As his clean swords hang
From his complicated belt
Of silver and gold.

I say he inspires
Love or hatred in me

And I sing this
Out of praise for his regal folly

Before a girl lies in his bed
He will kneel into his own blood

Before he is tenderly laid
The ravens will get him

This friend of the prince
Will end under crows

Where

When

This one son of Mario?

A mind that lives between two languages

Is never made up

And as a preparation for death

That is no bad thing.

Now you are equal with the wisdom of the ages

The libraries of time have no more shelves

Eternity is one book

Without numbered pages

Where the words sing in any colour

And minds are never made up.

# LINES ON AN
# UNSUCCESSFUL POLITICIAN

He trained himself to engrave the air
With promises: they brought no fire
From heaven. His speeches
Evaporated under the soft pressures
Of the prevailing wind.

He attended trends: measured
Opinions; waited
As the less gifted filled
Dead men's shoes.

The call never came. Why
Should it his wife said
And he mourned inwardly
The fierce mother who planted
The urge to office
In an eager heart.

Nothing to copy in space
Only count the stars
Said the five dead fingers

Poets in orbit
Compose and sing in circles
Only bright elegies

For old relations
Striking new claims
Like meteoric stakes
In the planet's heart.

At the window of the ward
My soul sits waiting
Observing the last contortions
Of the body that contained
And cherished it
With a curious detachment.

It was all imagination but
It doesn't seem to worry
About the pained dissolution
Or where it will go or who else
Will cherish and absorb it
When this body's last
Spasm of revolt against
The state of nothing is over.

I have a soul, I call it
Imagination. It sits on
The hospital window sill
And observes the last con-
tortions of its body with
A curious detachment.

When the pain and the dissolution
Are complete where
Will it go when my last
Spasm of revolt against
The state of nothing is over?

It may hang around
A flaw in the glass
Purged underfoot still
But refracting the past
Mutations of light
For anyone who cares
To look, light-like
Music without words.

# A TIME BEFORE

There was a time before
We gave names to things
We were naturally generous
The walls of the world were wide
Enough for us to share the morning
What went on
Was beyond words and numbers
Stretching between trees
To reach no horizon
And no gate.

Until we built one
And created the world outside
All words inherited by hostile
Creatures who dared to mirror
Our gestures of possessions
And delight.

Was it at that point
The source of our being
Turned cold and unforgiving.

Into the cage of old age
We imagine
The days pass
And we stay.
In reality
We pass
And the days stay
Ungrieving
Not bothered
To look where
We've gone.

A wordless world not silent. Trees
Secrete their own musical
Notation. Grass in all its forms
Insists on singing just as
Nettles sting. Birds and beasts
Burst out their own intuitive choruses. The air
Controls the clouds
And holds back on high
The single word
That alone contains our
End and our beginning.

# GOVERNING CLASS

Do we miss them
As we bolt the doors at night
And switch the terrors of the street
Into a coloured bottle.

They always judged their lives important
Buying gold fillings for their teeth
Migrating south when the spiders tired
Of weaving spells in their sullen orchards.

In the winter villas as the winter winds turned up
They added codicils to their wills before wood fires
Seeing in the flames reflections of their former glories
Weighing up their worth, projecting memories.

Buoyed up by visits from expectant relatives
So that out of office they could keep up
A lifetime's habit of deeply respecting themselves

Ah the burden of office the penalty of power
Those lurid dreams of native riots being forced
To listen to hymns of hate face children
Spitting at them in the streets

For the sake of becoming icons, statues
Hiding between the oleanders gazing
Sightless at the sunset on the property rocks
Was it all worth it? By god it was.

# FLOOR LITTER

No story left to tell, the floor
Is littered with blocks of letters
Someone else can clear up
Bedtime in a house scheduled
For demolition the windows already gone
Dreams of inconsequence drift
In a cold and incurious air
No story left to tell.

If nobody cares you can fly
Higher in the cage even the
Bars seem to expand made as they are
Of appetites strengthened with
Irony and Self Regard.

How many miles from this
Distemper to Jupiter's moon
Measured that is in sharp
Didactic mode: ask the poet
Who hides inside the storm
Measure the immeasurable, make
A whole canto where space said
Nothing lives in this cold hole.

# HOMEWORK

Who does history belong to, said the adolescent
Wriggling above her homework
The Goth when he rode in
Theodoric when he strangled the historian
Jefferson when he dreamt of a canal
And more and more navigation westward.

Random reflections. Every seventh year
Let the deserts be reassessed
And the bones moved out of the oldest tombs

Whose history indeed but yours
Emerging angel. Such dust as it rises
Will become the transient bloom on your cheeks.

And when you are old
Will come to rest like a pinpoint of magic
Enduring music in your eyes.
The Past is the safest place
Every door on the far side of an eyelid.

'Why do birds sing?'
We heard the old woman answer her own question.
She sat on her kitchen chair blinking in the sun
'I too am a living substance. People here know me
The *Principe* shows me respect
He calls me *Cara signora*. So why
should this woman my only son married
Pray for my death?'

She wanted to speak
And for our part we did her
                    the kindness to listen.
She had invited us into her garden
Telling us to help ourselves to the figs.
She no longer had the strength to pick them.

The geraniums in their pots looked after themselves
Her quarters were under the shadow of the castle
The land up to the ruined gate was hers
And the view of the lake and the sunlight.

'Piece by piece she empties my house'
                    the old woman said
'I am eighty seven. What can I do about it?
He lets her take what she likes. Besotted by her
And yet I had to force him to marry her.
                    Can you understand that?'

We gathered the figs in three baskets
Murmuring our sympathy.
Hens scratched about under the olive trees
What was left of her from war was draped in
                                  unrelieved black
Her face was shrivelled and helpless. Her hands
Lay like a wreath on her empty lap.

What shall I call her? Proverbs are little use to me
Although I know so many. I could attack her
With turns of phrase, idioms she's never heard of
But what would be the use if he slunk away
As if it all did not concern him
Burying his curly head in his drawings and papers.

'I adopted him when he was three months old
God had decided not to give me a son
After I visited the emperor's spring for barren women.
We doted on him. Luigi too
My *contadino* husband brown as the earth

So hard of hand and like a season slow moving
He was clever. His voice more beautiful than a bird's
His cheeks smoother than apples
His eyelashes longer than any girl's.

# INFLAMMATORY STUFF

Burn the royal yacht.
The student was quite serious when he said it
He overlooked the fact that the vessel
Was five miles out to sea
Impregnable with water
He himself was already burning
With centuries of injustice.

You can't spell it let alone burn it
His academic tutor jeered
This added fuel to the flames
It pulled the handle of the fruit machine
And three lemons came up
Shaped like hand grenades

Violence will get you nowhere
The academic peered in his coffee cup
Take advantage of the academic process.

# TWO OF EVERYTHING

While the previous state still exists
Not over there but in this field
Change cannot occur. Neither you
Nor anyone else can be dead
And alive at the same time.
That seems obvious enough: nevertheless
Yesterday or the day before or today
It takes some proving. Change
Said Aristotle owns its own
Space and Time and between two moments
There is always time.

So when did you change
From nothing into you and at
What point did your embryo
And your soul set up house?
Does there have to be two of everything?

Mind where you tread: the past
Is broken glass: the universe
Contrary to adolescent expec-
Ation is not phallocentric

And life as the terrible virgins mumbled
Is an accident waiting to happen
But once the collision occurs
It's no accident: so look out
Embrace the accomplished fact.

Don't talk about doing it
Do it. The consummation
Or whatever you like to call it
Is a ritual beyond language.

Save your words for prayers
So that in the fullness of time
Dressed up in dog Latin
The worm in the bud
May acquire the words
And sing out the meaning.

Jumping on tables, flagrant
Exhibitionism is a practice
With diminishing returns.
Learn to reserve and register
Observations. Be what you are
Just another face in the crowd.

# BEING RATIONAL

The rational resents the irrational
Patently. So what have we in common
A language in which words
Are two faced like coins that turn
In slow motion between the apex
And the radius of the spin.

Look at it this way, brother, comrade
So that we can at last smile
At the same gyrations of a clown
Who balances an empty globe
On his forehead and dances like an angel
On the blunt head of a magical
Presence suspended for no apparent reason
In the quarters we have to share in the winter
Solstice of our joint existence.

# DOMESTIC SCENE

A silent film not a woodcut
Unfolds in the sunlit garden
And we watch through the double glazed window

The mother young and calm reclines in the camp bed
Reversing the roles so that the two
Little daughters attend her with
Plastic toys and invisible cakes
Magic medicine mixed from leaves
And flowers. They also bring daisy chains
To hang about her neck.

Above their heads as they play
The wisteria blooms and the rosebuds
Wait to open.
From the kitchen comes the clatter of pots.

For what purpose these signals
A brain with thoughts
Fluttering at the last gasp
Fingering civilisations flitting
Like a dying moth around
The gloomy biosphere.

So many lives broken
Stiffening in a human silence

What kind of a poet was
He like anyone else

Under arrest
                    stumbling
Not pushed and shoved
                              down
                                             six
                                                    steps
Into the bare cell
Like anywhere else
                              With blood
Stained walls like anyone
Else breathing broken
Defiance
          broken iambics
Nothing to write with

Having backed
The wrong side, there was no remission.

That cell those stains
As dead as the mood
And the man singing
In the solar wind
His own perishable elegy.

A broken American Memory
Turning in space here
A dead missile
In search of the heart of silence.

# PADDINGTON

I walked in a drunken stupor of holiness
Towards Paddington Station at four o'clock on a Friday afternoon
There was no train and I had no share
In the world's soft Treasures of glittering Joys.
To distract my mind from the distinguished clothes of wickedness
Or the spilled beer of Despair.

'Will it do you any good?' he said
(He was the very smart Tempter)
'I have failed again, can you help me, please can you help me?'
Stared out of my friend Despair.

I fled from them both at four o' clock
Because my feet could negotiate the metropolitan quicksand
Only in the sunny morning, buoyant with sunshine, but never
As the day wore on
And the telephones continued to cry in the gathering dark.

That pregnant moment
When your loaded brush
Struck the canvas
Time sank into a blue moment
A day an afternoon
Around the trembling brush
Defined a segment of
Eternity and you are gone
Your skilful hand
Crumbling
Only that moment living
A startled echo of
The votive urge towards eternity.

# ANOTHER ROUTE

Perception out of pain
Is that the only gate?
The spring that forces smiles
On the most sullen face
Offers another route
But not a governed state
Something against the grain
Makes a riddling universe plain.

# COMPUTING

Computers write now
Compose menus
And poems stuffed with
Difficult words

They are not so good
At singing yet
But that will come

Meanwhile blood
Provides me with
An indefinable rejoicing
But no words yet
To encompass the explosion.

# DICTIONARIES

Access by language only
Here the Pillars of Hercules
Are dictionaries
Washed with usage

Let me voyage on
There may be risk
In the short vigil that remains

It is in the other mind
The untouched world
beyond the sun
Resides

There too the sums of solitude
Can be transposed
Metamorphosis and music.

Anyone but everyone can operate
The theology of selfishness
That accident beloved of fabulists
And heretics: you were one in a million
When the sperm and the egg made
Their chance encounter and the freehold
Stays with you like breath
And even before that or even after
The responsibility was yours and
The reckoning was due sooner or later.

The tired writer with swollen feet
Leans over as you pay up your privilege
Dear me has to be sorry for him too.
Fate can't be fate if it's a series of explosive surprises.

# A REHEARSAL

Who said the tomb is the rehearsal
Room of heaven? I did. In that
Case it should be published in
The college gazette. The processes of
Nature are fulfilled. The individual
Nature is transformed. That could
Go in two styles. I must concentrate
On the single spot and meditate until
The spark from heaven falls
Or at least value the solution
I could not ask for more.

# AN ACTRESS

Earthbound the stage
Is nailed to the floor
Down those glittering stairs
Direct from heaven she comes, spotlit,
With a female swagger
Artificial starlight in her eyes

This is not her essence
Only the immanence of her art
Which is illumination
Through illusion

She lives inside, shy,
Rare as a dying species
Held together by
The expectation of love

Not to take exactly
But to give with the excess
Of an island sunlight

The shores of assembled islands
Lie in wait for her white feet.

# AGOSTINO

The labour of others is graceful
One's own can be hardship
Agostino works amongst his vines
His wife Elisa hoes the soil around the olive trees
His motorbike lies under the cherry tree
This scythe needs sharpening
This is my sixty-second year.

The day he was sixty-two
Marco stared through the window
As if he were seeing the starkness of it all
His tenure coming to an end
The castle crumbling
And underneath
Young German students excavating
Etruscan tombs.

# THE STABLE

In the attic of the universe
Doubt is everything. Volcanoes
Keep their distance. The solar system
Is a model of restraint

But in this fevered parlour
Possessive love and hatred
Revenge and moral indignation

Buzz like generations
Of horseflies trapped
In the wrong stable.

We suffer inside
An invisible storm.

# HONESTY

Honesty is always painful he assured me
When his inclination to the brutal truth
Had been tamed and purified. The fee
He charged more than covered the expenses
Of an unruffled lifestyle. My plea
To debit by instalments he graciously
Allowed. Now I clean his boots
Correct his proofs and deal with his women
When they scream for some consideration
By comfortably lying
What else can you do as you stand there
Listening to them crying.

What you live in
Is you. Plainly
A thin
Skin a thick
Skull.

Between
Air and
Sea
Earth
To lie in

No audience
Worms
Singing fingering
You and the silence.

'Explain it again', his wife said, 'It was a dream'
He said. 'That's no explanation!' she said

'Imagine a small eisteddfod where
The local talent which means almost everybody
Reenact the first mistakes of the race
Like a challenge solo: I gave the prize

To the lonely one who started out
In a time of war without documents
Or a ticket or a destination without
Locking the leather valise of her Fortune
Only a certain Arthur in her shadow
Limping along to catch her murmuring
His irrelevant praises: too tired
To coin new phrases or hang on
How shall I put it to the time honoured
Syllables as they drop like the teeth of
A broken comb all over the wet pavement.'

Inside his wicker skeleton
He shivers at the prospect of another spring
His brain may bounce about
Sustained by friction, his bones
Know better. His inefficient mouth
Dribbles gratitude, his skin
Suppurates discontent and fails
To wrap itself for comfort around
Cold bones.

# THE SECRET

With genuine interest she inquired
When did you acquire
The habit of living
Weightless with words in your head?

It began early under a table
While a storm broke overhead
Adults in anger; tumults
That made the air tremble
Doors banging walls of restraint
Collapsing and bookshelves the last sheltering fable

So it goes on no scalpel can uncover
Inside the shape of living lies a secret
Nothing can uncover.

# THE FLY

How long does it take a word
To fill or fit into its right time and
Place in *l'oeuvre*
Since it's all outside time
Who is there to be counting
All the same longer if you dither
Like a fly between the decay
Of two languages.

# AN OPEN SECRET

The minister plenipotentiary has no place in fiction.
Steadily exclude him, although you know he's there,
The open secret, gaping under the archway
Like an open grave.

Take the day at *Norcia*. Europeans at their best behaved
We carried our needs in our rucksacks
Used stout sticks, forded rivers and torrent beds
Penetrating the *burrone* where the birds sang
Their own *Te Deum* and the leaves like an instant
Population explosion sprang up to the sun.

The tombs were not easy to find. 'Overgrown'
You said. What grows in a tomb? The robbers
Looked for treasure and the weather defaced
The carving on the *tufa*. What did the symbols represent?
Were the letters read from right to left
Or vice versa. Which came first? Birth or Death.
Certainly you can't have one without the other

Muscles are needed in the mind as in the arm
And skill in the fingers of the brain
Designs intricate patterns and threads spun from experience.
Prose is a looser texture for long distance runners not acrobats.

# THE MARBLE TOMB

Was it a miracle or a willing suspension of belief?
We stood by his great uncle's unused tomb
And the October sunlight as Bremiante had arranged it
Over the faithful (how can I call them a congregation?)
The smart Milanese, ready to enjoy the best of both worlds
But at this moment more solemn than sceptical
Not listening to the Dominican's oratory
More than was necessary to carry his arguments
As lightly as the stirrup ... bore in the shadow of bad ottocento painting,
While their loving eyes watched the green priest
Perform grim magic on the High Altar
With firmness and discretion.
Why should I demand that the cross in the sunlight should spout blood
Or the church be restored by a genuine collection
And not a rich man's gift in exchange for a marble tomb?
Was it blood? Nobody tasted it and nobody knew
For me, however, it was always the same answer:
The word would speak when the word was flesh again.

# BONES

Can these be Boethius' bones?
Were they human? The sarcophagus
Was certainly made by human hands.
Digits held the hammer and before that
The pencil that traced out the design.

He seems captured somehow. Theodoric may have killed him
But the church down the ages has him captured
Saved from the heretic ferocity of the Goths
And of the mother church's eternal power that rests
Like his sarcophagus
On the cold altar stone.
Keep looking,
Nothing but sacrifice will do the trick.

# LOVESONG

Who am I who was she
Something or nothing
According to the magnitude of our illusions.
She stepped out of a place and time
Like a goddess out of the water
And each drop that clings to her skin
Was a contamination.

So it has always been.
Our skins are toughened by contact
Not with other skins but with
The invisible acids of these days

These are real clothes
The vestments of pollution

They make us what we are
And puzzle our descendants

Augustine of Hippo records
As he moaned before shedding his skin
Each age and therefore each
Second of existence are
Equidistant from eternity

And in this only lies our hope
My dear our so called undying affection
Is the mote in the beam

Of this love that controls the planet
And holds the sun in its place.

Our love was comforting
So why should you go before me?
Even a withered leaf has form
Beautiful when held up to the sun.

# THE SHADOW FALLS

Who or what does a man represent
As his mind revolves and his shadow falls
On a rock he knows represents so many
Million years and when he knows

The rock of ages is only cosmic blows
Solidified by thermonuclear brush strokes
Into a tender gesture. This very corner
Overlooking the bay where the boat sails
Pale blue water stood its ground aeons
Before his shadow bent into a question
As another of matter who am I?

If the answer is *nessuno neb*
A Mister Nobody why do I respond
To my own voice and talk aloud
In the hope of being overheard.

The space I fill
The space I see
Was earmarked for me
Before the flood

Before the cosmic *modd*
The switched state of matter
To release the source
Of adolescent laughter.

As I wait to shrink and not exist

You recognise my dream

And song of galaxies

Are one diminished seventh

Of what was once called heaven.

# EVENING

As the fire dies
As echo sinks
Into the well of silence
Time trembles
On its slender axis
Past and future flutter
In each other's faces
Like the transparent petals
Of an unplucked flower.

# WHY WATER WON'T BEND

*'Cyflwr Dŵr'*

Does water fret about its wet condition?
Assume it contains a liquid soul, a single eye
Flowing, a tear unable to distinguish
Between an end and a beginning,
A fluid longing for an instrument
Like the knife of time that whittles flesh
And tempers character: that withers lips
Commands leaves to drop from trees
Like paratroopers under fire:
A frantic search for the element that could tame
That ceaseless motion,
Provide a method to embrace and not drown
The truth of things.

# ULTIMATE DISCOVERIES

Ultimate discoveries
Are made in winter
Snow on the piste
And galaxies piercing the sky
Pin pricks in the velvet
Choreograph small lives
With giant steps expose
Eyes in exile with distance
That defies celebration
How far is far when it
Embraces near?

But this is summer: the sounds of the world
Are drifting in through open windows
As familiar as handwriting
With the same hint of truth
Acting to manifest itself
Through a notation of silence.

Whatever came into existence
In that mythic winter
Persists: a spider's thread
Of existence suspended
Like a piece of debris in outer space
That intermittently catches the sun
And threatens the sky with
The glitter of inexplicable messages.

The twilight for an old man
Is a procession of spectres
They come sliding in, shy
And familiar, tics and gestures
Smiles in the doorway of the mind
Hands raised and sweetly balanced
Between resurrection
And dissolution.

Outside the narrow door
Lies darkness and the three spinsters
These are tunnels should you
Need to travel and a choice of guides
From one safe haven to another
Faces you never touch voices
That carry meaning
More penetrative than words.

The boat was sailing and the day was new
I ran and my impatience grew
I ran and my strength was born anew
The garden sunshine glittered on the dew
I ran, but as I ran the sun ran too
The sundial shadow fell, *byr yw byw*.

# TRIUMPH OF OLD AGE

To accept the rough embrace
Of the seasons and be at one
With the delicacy of the world.

Reduce to residual silence
An old man takes an
Animal view of the world
A bird
Shoots out of an August
Hedge and takes part of him
With her above white faced
Cattle browsing on his behalf.

His life lingers among
The living housed
And fed friendly hands
Guide sustenance
His mouth, his mind
Floats less lonely
Than a single
Cloud in a blue sky.

There is a delicacy
That belongs this green
Island that survives
The rough embrace of the seasons
And in this late August
Presents this oneness

With the word
As a passing sunlight
Sweeps down
With the warmth of silence
The triumph of old age.

# THE OLD COUPLE

Sleep in the afternoon
Descends like soot
From a chimney
Larger than life.

Don't resist it, Wisdom
Can live in narrow houses
When love lies under the dust
To be recovered with a soft brush.

My hands have aged
So have I, Skin has its own metaphysics
Beyond spoken magic

Words talk of iron fingers
But our mute palms
Are points of entry
To a different landscape.

Your vigilance is a virtue
Not a blemish. The remainder
Of our journey is both
Departure and arrival.

We travel without passport
Our steps are shorter
But the same footfall
Will deliver untrodden paths

Towards perpetual refreshment
In that place of light
Furnished by the ancient of days.